THE
C.R.M. POCKETI

By David Alexander and Ch

Drawings by Phil Hailstone

"Brilliant and inspiring even for an organisation that has focused on building long-term profitable customer relationships, this book sets the context for the next Millennium."
Mike Norris, Chief Executive, Computacenter plc

"Concise but comprehensive. This book will help you capture the imagination and support of all parts of your organisation. A must for any disciple of CRM."
Nigel Grimes, Director of Customer Strategy, Centrica

CONTENTS

CONTENTS

AUTHORS' INTRODUCTION

What to expect in this book

We are living in an increasingly competitive and rapidly changing environment where it is more difficult to acquire, retain and develop customers profitably. Who can doubt that the right customers are vital to your business's success? Customer Relationship Management (CRM) strategies should now be the driving force for cross-functional teamwork, both inside and outside the organisation, to improve the business.

This book will help you understand what Customer Relationship Management is all about, from a strategic level through to practical implementation. An effective CRM strategy can deliver outstanding improvements in profitability, revenue growth and sustainability of the business.

Any organisation with customers of whatever type will benefit from this book.

WHAT IS CUSTOMER RELATIONSHIP MANAGEMENT?

Customer Relationship Management (CRM) is about delivering:
- Increased Economic Value Add (EVA)*
- Increased revenue and profit

Through knowledge and understanding of:
- Who your customers are
- How they interact with your business today
- How they wish to interact with your business in the future
- How valuable and profitable they are to you
- What their future value is to you

By enabling you to make informed decisions about:
- Overall business strategy for your organisation
- Which customers you should acquire and develop
- What services or products you should develop, acquire or provide
- What channels you need to support and develop
- How to focus/organise your business to deliver operational excellence aligned to the strategy

A way of analysing what to invest in by assessing what offers the best return on resources of all types (people, money, time, etc)

DRIVERS FOR CUSTOMER
RELATIONSHIP MANAGEMENT

DRIVERS FOR CUSTOMER RELATIONSHIP MANAGEMENT

INTRODUCTION

CRM provides an effective framework for understanding and dealing with a wide range of internal/external pressures affecting the success of you and your organisation today. This section looks at the main issues affecting relationships with your customers, and provides a checklist of questions to address and points to consider:

- The competitive landscape and the pressures it places on you. What's your response?

- Changes in the way your organisation is being valued. How are you addressing this?

- Customers in the future will be different. Their expectations and knowledge are increasing exponentially. Have you analysed these trends? How do you respond and what changes will you make to address this?

- Do you know about the serial switchers? How do you spot them and stop them from dragging your business performance down?

- The economic landscape is changing. How will this affect you and what is your response?

- Technology is changing; it can make or break you. Have you assessed it? How do you harness it and integrate it into your business to deliver tangible benefits?

COMPETITIVE LANDSCAPE, CHANGE, CONFLICTS OF INTEREST

This could be your greatest threat, or source of best intelligence and advantage.

- Increased competition and reduced margins - *How will you respond?*
  - new players with lower transaction costs and streamlined business models
  - comparison between offers completed in seconds
  - lack of control of the sales cycle

- Change is the only constant; pace of change increasing - *How flexible are you?*
  - need to rapidly respond
  - return on investment harder to achieve
  - short lifetime value of products and services

CHANGES IN WAY ORGANISATIONS ARE VALUED

Conflicts regarding how a business is measured and valued - by the stockmarket, shareholders, management, employees, customers, suppliers and partners - raise new challenges. How do you measure and communicate your value?

Traditional model:
- Fixed assets
- Current assets
- Liabilities
- Inventory
- Goodwill/brands and products
- Quarterly/half-yearly and annual results

New model will include:
- Number of customers
- Metrics of customer value
- Share of customers' spend
- Customer databases
- Predicted customer lifetime values
- Benchmarking

New model will emphasise:
- Future value and profitability of existing customers
- Ability to find new customers who fit the profile of good customers

CUSTOMER EXPECTATIONS

- Your customers demand an integrated multi-channel service and more control:
  - call centres, web, mobile phones, retail, mail order, interactive TV
  - access from anywhere, anytime to suit their needs 24 hours a day
  - immediate gratification and fulfilment

- Your customers have less time and they are assaulted on all sides by competitive offers

- Their satisfaction is not a guarantee of loyalty or repeat business for you

- Do not confuse loyalty with complacency as prime reason for retaining customers

- Your customers may have few barriers to prevent them changing to someone else:
  - easy, pain-free switching from one supplier to another is a common selling feature
  - obvious examples are: the utilities such as electricity, gas and telecommunications; financial services such as mortgage providers and credit card companies; suppliers of commodity products such as stationery; and supermarkets

CUSTOMER KNOWLEDGE IS INCREASING EXPONENTIALLY

The customer's ability to analyse your offerings and those of your competitors, and to make a decision without even speaking to you or your competitors, results in loss of control of the traditional sales cycle.

- Growth of information available from many sources including media, internet and specialist interest groups

- Every customer can be an expert - customer's knowledge can easily be greater than some front line staff

- The acceptable gap between customer expectation and actual quality of service or product delivered is shrinking

- Media is driving customers to 'think and consider' rather than consume

- Internet is reducing some goods and services to commodity pricing where value is not articulated

DRIVERS FOR CUSTOMER RELATIONSHIP MANAGEMENT

CUSTOMER OF THE FUTURE WILL BE DIFFERENT

The traditional customer - on whom much theory and business strategy is and has been based since World War II - is changing. CRM provides a framework for understanding who the customer was, is and will be in the future. Key trends are:

- Increased flexibility in working environment, formation of virtual organisations
- Changing demographics of traditional family unit
- Greater choice of channels and range of products/services on a global base
- Increased self-sufficiency
- Increased segmentation and isolation
- Life increasingly becomes a series of trade-offs
- Life events take over from life stages - planning based on groupings of child, young adult, adult, mature adult and retiree are no longer enough. Life events are more significant:
  - B2C: passing driving test, university attendance, degree, first job, redundancy, promotion, marriage, birth of children, divorce, second marriage, retirement
  - B2B: start company, enter top three in market, market leader, flotation, acquisitions, divestments, changes in CEO or senior management, major new customers and products

(7)

DRIVERS FOR CUSTOMER RELATIONSHIP MANAGEMENT

GUARD AGAINST COMING PLAGUE OF 'SERIAL SWITCHERS'

The symptom
Clever customers who switch from supplier to supplier on an ongoing basis to take advantage of special incentives and offers

The illusion
They meet company acquisition and competitive switching targets

The truth
They never contribute any profit because they never stay long enough with you to provide a return on investment. Don't forget, you carry heavy costs: acquisition, set-up/welcome, administration and exit costs

The cause
Lack of integration and analysis across the business allows bad decisions to be made

DRIVERS FOR CUSTOMER RELATIONSHIP MANAGEMENT

CONSIDER FUTURE ECONOMIC LANDSCAPE

The world is changing, giving rise to shifts in economic behaviour. Have you assessed how/when these will affect your customers and business? Will you take advantage or minimise risk?

- Traditional markets will give way to networks of connected interest. Traditional segmentation will not work:
  - customers will form their own groups (based on their interests/needs) on the internet and through clubs, eg: investment, education, health, sports and hobbies
  - grouping customers by age, family demographics, size of organisation or location is insufficient for basing your business strategy on
- Access to information, services and goods will shift to rental or right to use model. Ownership becomes a marginal activity, eg:
  - video/TV on demand rather than physical videos
  - access to online reports/newsletters rather than paper copies
  - renting a car for three years rather than buying one

DRIVERS FOR CUSTOMER RELATIONSHIP MANAGEMENT

CONSIDER FUTURE ECONOMIC LANDSCAPE

- Intellectual assets will become the primary thrust for growth and valuation:
    - ideas, concepts, designs, content, images, services, processes
    - eg: Nike's primary assets are its brand and design skills; most production/distribution is outsourced

- Buyers and sellers will physically meet less and less through greater use of call centres, internet and interactive TV

- Meteoric descent in transaction costs will make some traditional business processes obsolete. Organisations will fail if they do not evolve. When did you last compare your costs?

- Customers will be seeking *just in time* experiences

- A single person's life could be a market in its own right given that you have a range of products and services that can be supplied to them across their lifetime. Consider:
    - cradle to grave relationships were once the norm - why not now?
    - meeting the needs of a specific individual high-spending profitable customer

DRIVERS FOR CUSTOMER RELATIONSHIP MANAGEMENT

TECHNOLOGY MAKING DECISIONS

- Customers will empower technology to make decisions on their behalf
- Customers will set rules for software agents, who then act on them:
  - car of the future: reports service problems/accidents, buys petrol
  - house of the future: selects utility suppliers
  - purchasing agents: scour multiple channels (eg: the web, interactive TV and mobile services) for products and services to meet customer requests
  - auction agents: start bidding for products and services; dynamic pricing begins to take hold
- Brand will only count if the customer puts it in the rules book for the agent
- Software agents don't care about brands, direct marketing, human interaction or emotional support

DRIVERS FOR CUSTOMER RELATIONSHIP MANAGEMENT

KEY ISSUES FOR THE FUTURE

- The future value of your customers will be a critical factor in assessing the value of your business
- Traditional marketing models will not work for certain products and services in the future
- All of your customers are not equal, therefore the levels of service should be varied from customer to customer, depending on their value to your business - now and in future
- Only the requirements and expectations of your valued customers should be used to drive strategy development and investment
- Understanding why a customer is valuable to you and what they look like when first acquired will become a key capability in your business
- Successful organisations will develop processes designed to support their best customers and deliver value, not necessarily products and channels

FRAMEWORK FOR CUSTOMER RELATIONSHIP MANAGEMENT

BALANCE & INTEGRATION

In order to deliver an effective Customer Relationship Management Strategy it is vital to understand the full scope of business contributions and customer needs. This chapter outlines:

- Customer expectations
- Calculating future value of customers
- Agreeing business objectives and defining a strategy
- Creating an integrated cross-functional team
- Defining business processes
- Technology
- Marketing

CUSTOMERS' EXPECTATIONS

Customers' expectations are soaring. However, there are six key areas of customer needs that, if met, represent the ideal relationship for a customer:

Flexibility to meet their individual requirements

Deal with one person for the whole experience

Communication that is relevant to them

CUSTOMER

Telling an organisation information only once

Recognition for who they are - their history and potential

Easily obtained information at all customer interactions

Delivery of these key needs is the Customer Relationship Management challenge.

CALCULATING FUTURE CUSTOMER VALUE

- Delivering against your customers' wants and needs can add costs into your business as it may involve more and better staff, newer technologies, more support services, additional channels and speedier response times. **Can you afford it?**

- To maximise your profit it is necessary to differentiate your customers based on value, in order to meet your best customers' needs and make profit

- The premise going forward is that all your customers are not equal in their future value to your business - some will actually lose you money

- Therefore, customer lifetime value is the backbone of any CRM strategy:

  - Who should your organisation serve?
  - How should your organisation serve them?
  - What return on investment will you make?
  - Which of your customers does your organisation no longer wish to service?

VISION, OBJECTIVES & STRATEGY

Without a clear understanding of your customers and their needs you cannot define a vision for the business or set objectives and design strategies to meet them.

The question of stewardship versus leadership is important. Stewardship is all about maintaining the status quo. Traditionally, businesses have been measured on stewardship or short-term performance such as earnings per share, notional market share and annual growth compared with notional market growth rates. These types of measures do not articulate the true strength of a business and they drive behaviour to short-term tactics.

Leadership is about vision, motivation, creating momentum for change and growth in value for long-term success. Under stewardship innovation, investment and medium-to long-term thinking are seen as representing little or no value.

CRM strategies cannot exist in a leaderless vacuum where short-termism rules.

VISION, OBJECTIVES & STRATEGY

Today, customer objectives and value must be central to your business planning. It enables a more strategic approach to be taken in terms of creating a vision, setting objectives and defining a strategy to deliver them.

- Which customer groups will your business focus on?
    - Surely the ones that will deliver profit longer-term?
    - How will you grow the value and profitability of those groups?
    - How will your organisation exit from loss-making customers?
- What product and services deliver your best value customers?

Customer objectives must be met with a CRM strategy:

- What strategies across product, pricing, operations, channels, service and marketing will meet these objectives profitably?
- How does your organisation align itself to service the customer and meet the objectives?

FRAMEWORK FOR CRM

PROCESSES: DEFINE & INTEGRATE

An organisation that has clear vision, and has set customer-centric objectives and strategies, must review business processes and their integration into the business.

- Putting your customers at the centre means designing efficient processes around them to deliver the desired results.
- What processes do you need and which ones do you have? What changes will you make and what do you need to develop? What is the cost to retain and grow your most valuable customers?
- How do you make these processes seamless across the organisation?
- How do you know the total value of a customer across the whole organisation in order to trigger the right support?
- How do you move from a product-centric to a customer-centric model?

TECHNOLOGY: ORGANISATIONS TODAY

Traditionally, customers interacted with separate technology silos within a business. This created costly duplication, varying customer experiences and conflicting ways of dealing with the customer relationship.

The Customers/Markets

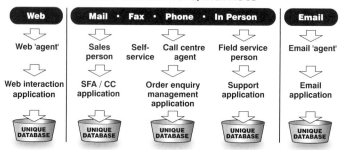

TECHNOLOGY: VISION FOR THE FUTURE

A CRM strategy seeks to use technology to bring together all customer interactions, thereby creating a seamless customer experience and achieving business economies.

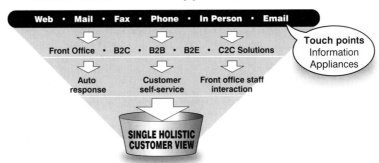

Staff / Customers / Suppliers / Markets

Web · Mail · Fax · Phone · In Person · Email

Front Office · B2C · B2B · B2E · C2C Solutions

Touch points
Information
Appliances

Auto response · Customer self-service · Front office staff interaction

SINGLE HOLISTIC CUSTOMER VIEW

STRENGTHEN CUSTOMER BONDS THROUGH RELATIONSHIP MARKETING

Your customers now interact, deal and speak with you across multiple different media channels - call centre, web, mobile phone, retail, mail order, interactive TV. A marketing strategy that utilises all of these channels to communicate with the right customers, at the right time, using the right channel is a key part of your CRM planning. This includes marketing strategies for:

- Gaining consistent customer knowledge
- Communicating the right messages to the right segments of your customers
- Utilising multi-channel response options
- Maximising support services for your most valuable customers
- Measuring for profit

CREATE AN INTEGRATED CRM PROGRAMME TEAM

CRM is a business strategy that cannot be handled by any single person or department within your company.

- Customers see your business as one entity, not separate units
- A customer's total experience with your company is influenced by many factors, from marketing and customer service through to operational delivery and effective service-enabling technology

It is essential, therefore, that a cross-functional team is assembled from the start to plan and implement an organisation-wide CRM strategy. This team should have:

- The best representatives from each department (you know who they are, do not accept anything less than the best)
- The support of the CEO who should be able to explain the strategy

NOTES

DIFFERING CRM THEMES & START POINTS

ONE SIZE DOES NOT FIT ALL

Many organisations work across multiple markets, each with specific needs and some common needs. This chapter deals with the two major CRM themes and start points of today. They apply equally well to commercial, public sector and not-for-profit organisations.

Business to Business CRM definition

An organisation trades goods/services with another organisation over an extended period of time, either on an ad hoc or on-going basis. The supplier may represent a key component in the customer's supply chain or support services for the delivery of the customer's own business with its clients.

Business to Consumer CRM definition

An organisation sells goods/services to a citizen either through direct or indirect channels.

Some organisations can operate both themes. Other themes exist such as Business to Employee, Citizen to Citizen, Business to Supplier and Business to Partner. All are variations and augmentations on the two lead themes.

BUSINESS TO BUSINESS CRM

B2B CRM is about sharing knowledge and creating a common understanding of markets, competitors, prospects and customers in order to:

- Sell more, reduce cost and increase profit

It enables you to translate strategy into action:

- Focus on key business opportunities
- Reduce transaction costs
- Increase customer dependency
  - better, more personal experience
  - easier to do business with
- Provide the right information to the right people at the right time

TYPICAL B2B CRM CONTENT

The information needed to manage business to business relationships is more extensive, in both range and depth, than is traditionally seen in the business to consumer model. Key groupings are:

- Market/segment information
- Organisation profile
- Sales account information and bid planning
- Contract and service level agreements
- Revenue and margin details
- Contacts and profiles
- New product development/improvement
- Support

Each of these is covered in the following pages. They will act as a checklist during planning and preparation for a CRM programme.

DIFFERING CRM THEMES & START POINTS

MARKET/SEGMENT INFORMATION

The environment in which your customer's business operates is key to:
- Understanding your customer from an overall trend perspective
- Benchmarking your customer's behaviour to market norms
- Appreciating who your customer competes with

This knowledge aids understanding of what drives your customers. Ensure you know:
- What your customers buy
  - when, where and why
- The size and trend of their market/segment
  - their compound annual growth rate as a business
  - market intelligence on key issues affecting them (eg: government policy, legislation, market trend, City forecasts, new technologies)
- Competitor details
  - names; likely mergers
  - suppliers (Do you supply any of them and, if so, are you a specialist?)

ORGANISATION PROFILE

Any organisation can operate in a market. It will have its own culture, rules, strengths, weaknesses and ways of measuring itself. It is critical to understand these elements when communicating and planning effective CRM strategies. Typical questions to address are:

- What do your business customers do? Who are their customers? How are they positioned in their market? What are their current business objectives and strategy? You can find this information:
  - on websites, in their presentations, collateral, press releases, case studies, annual reports and accounts and by simply talking with them
  - in market reports, press articles, trade publications and a wealth of online news services
- What are their cultural styles and organisational structure?
  - physical, political, geographical, matrix - who makes decisions, why?
- What 'metrics' do they measure themselves by?
  - profit and loss, balance sheet, earnings per share, earnings per employee, number of customers, average revenue per customer, market share

SALES ACCOUNT INFORMATION

How does your organisation navigate customer information? Clearly, a unique reference number or code that ties it all together should be a prerequisite. In the sales account area you should have a way of linking what is in the process of being sold to what is ordered and what is delivered, through to what gets invoiced and subsequently supported. Key areas to check out are:

- **Sales ledger ID** - Is it unique?
- **Sales orders** - What is ordered
- **Specifications** - What needs to be delivered
- **Dispatches/tracking** - Where it is in the delivery cycle
- **Internal account team** - Who is involved with servicing and supporting this customer (sales, delivery and support personnel such as credit control, customer service, production, pre-sales, bid team members)

CONTRACTUAL OBLIGATIONS - DIFFERENCE BETWEEN PROFIT OR LOSS?

Many organisations spend a lot of time devising contracts and service agreements that are then filed and not communicated across the organisation. 'Walking the sales talk' is key to effective CRM strategy. To do this it is essential the following information is integrated into the business otherwise you can find yourself losing money fast:

- Contract ID - Is this linked to the sales ledger ID and can you track a contract?
- Business unit - Who sold it, who is delivering/supporting it?
- Terms and conditions - What did you commit to, by when?
- Service level agreements - What do you have to do, by when, how often and where?
- Penalties - What happens if you fail, how much exposure does your business have, can you afford it, will it happen?
- Start and end dates - How long did you commit to, have you renewed your contract or are you doing it for free, how do you track it?
- Product schedules - Did you make commitment dependent on new product/service development, is it still being developed and is it within the contract timescale?

FINANCIAL DETAIL

Once you have the business, how do you track the client's performance and your own across key areas? Understanding the customer from a financial perspective can highlight risk and opportunity. It provides a balance to other inputs from sales, marketing, support and delivery perspectives. Key areas are:

- **Historical revenue and margin** - Do you understand these indicators for each account, product, project, contract, ad hoc work and operational period? Can you spot trends in terms of value, mix and type of engagement?

- **Revenue projections** - What is the customer's forward commitment to your business over the coming years?

- **Invoice, credit history and credit rating** - How well do your customers pay, what is the value of their average invoice compared to your best customers, what does the rating agency say, how likely are they to pay, can they afford it?

- **Outstanding money owed** - How much do they owe, is the trend up or down, are they good payers, what does it cost if they are bad payers, is this a sign of problems with your service or their finances?

CONTACT INFORMATION

This is an area your organisation may well have focused on. But have you ended up with disjointed or multiple information sources? It is critical to build towards the concept of a single view of a customer and the contacts within your organisation. In this way everyone contributes to and benefits from building an effective profile. The key areas are:

- Full name, addresses
- History of roles performed, previous career history
- Telephone, e-mail, fax and web addresses
- Likes, dislikes, hobbies, family information
- Their relative position, and political affiliations and influence within the organisation (Who do they report to, work with, influence?)

NEW BUSINESS DEVELOPMENT

Understanding what potential business you have under development is a key indicator of the relative health of the business and likely demand on resources. With effective integration of information and communication you can make dramatic improvements in business planning and strategic decision-making. Focus on:

- **Quotations** - Who have you quoted, for what, how long are the quotations valid for, what profit will you make?

- **Bid information** - What business are you bidding for, what will you be selling and delivering, what are the risks?

- **Revenue forecasts** - When will orders be secured and need to be delivered?

- **Product forecasts** - When will the product be ready for marketing and delivery?

- **Suppliers** - Who are the customer's other suppliers and for what, how are you positioned, how do you defeat them?

- **Sales campaign planning and management** - What do you need to do to win and how do you go about it, how are you politically aligned?

SUPPORT INFORMATION

Through lack of knowledge, many organisations continue to support customers who are no longer paying for the service. The impact on paying customers can be highly damaging when they are held in a queue just behind a non-paying customer. The information needed is vast depending on your business. However, some common themes arise:

- **Supported product or service** - model, parts, quantity, location, serial or asset numbers, contract ID, warranty details, supplier details

- **Performance history of supported item** - comparative analysis covering mean time between component failure reports, number of support calls and types of issues raised

- **Access to knowledge bases** - use solutions from previous problems resolved, make technical/policy information available when people need it

- **Key performance indicators** - linked to service level obligations and assumed costs to deliver, allow monitoring of business performance dynamically

- **Resource allocation** - service centre(s) and support people involved aid assignment and planning of services

Get this area right and you can improve profitability significantly.

NEW PRODUCT DEVELOPMENT/IMPROVEMENT

Amazingly, many organisations fail to close the loop with their customers and the development teams who work tirelessly to bring new products and services to the market. Developers frequently only hear about problems, not future wishes. CRM closes the loop.

A CRM strategy will improve the results of the new/enhanced product or service (faster time to market, improved customer satisfaction, etc). Typically, it will address:

- **Focus groups** - Capture the output of these sessions within the CRM framework (ensure you are working with the right customer and prospective customer groups, those who will deliver future value)

- **Research material** - Focused on areas in line with strategy and target customers, can be made available to all people involved in developing customer relationship

- **Requirements capture** - Structured means of linking requirements to customer support issues and focus group output, enabling tracking of compliance of products/services to these needs

- **Service history and patterns** - Aid removal of defects in products/services and support continuous quality/process improvement (designing right first time in future)

BUSINESS TO CONSUMER CRM

In theory Business to Consumer CRM is much simpler than Business to Business CRM. Companies have relationships with one individual or a family group as opposed to multi-level relationships. Whilst many of the principles outlined previously apply, Business to Consumer CRM has some distinct differences:

- Consumer markets are much larger - some companies have millions of customers

- Buying process is faster and more dynamic

- Revenue from each customer is less and generates less profit per sale

- Often more difficult to distinguish between profitable and unprofitable customers

- Normally difficult to de-select non-profitable customers (seen as unacceptable)

- Some organisations don't have direct customer relationships (the relationship is with the brand which poses B2B type challenges)

- Biggest challenge in a competitive marketplace is to serve the right customers, with the right products and support services at the right time

THE CONSUMER BUYING PROCESS

Customers tend to be more fickle and less loyal than in a Business to Business context. In part this is because of the buying process which is:

- More frequent
- Quicker - sometimes people buy on impulse
- Subject to much more choice - many comparable products and services
- Subject to a single decision - made by one person or, at most, a family unit
- More transactional - buying rather than being directly sold to
- Less complicated - to fulfil orders

TYPICAL B2C CRM CONTENT

The breadth of information required is less than within a B2B CRM setting. Conversely, the volume of data naturally generated as part of trading tends to be greater, often resulting in data indigestion. For example, a supermarket chain with seven million customers who buy 40 different items once a week would have 14,000 million lines of transactional information in one year alone.

Information should only be collected and held if it can be used to make informed business decisions. In common with B2B CRM information needs, focus on financial, support, sales and contract details. Additionally, concentrate on:

- Individual customer contact details
- Segmentation and predictive modelling

DIFFERING CRM THEMES & START POINTS

INDIVIDUAL INFORMATION

Every end customer has their own DNA that makes them unique. Although rarely profitable to tailor-make solutions for each customer, it is helpful to segment customers according to their DNA. Seek this information:

- Name and home address
- Business address and job title
- Telephone, e-mail, fax and web details
- Current and historic ownership of products/services
- Key purchase dates (eg: home insurance one month before policy ends)
- Income (can they afford your goods/services?)
- Family composition

Also, track life events of the customer such as: passing driving test, university entrance, starting work, holiday, buying property, marriage, birth of children, investing in stocks and shares, divorce, redundancy, retirement, major health interventions.

DIFFERING CRM THEMES & START POINTS

SEGMENTATION

Segmentation and predictive modelling are key drivers in determining those customers you should acquire, those you should retain and those you should develop.

Segmentation is about analysing your customer base and putting customers into different categories according to distinct characteristics (DNA). Additionally, segments can be formed based on:

- **Recency** - how recently customers have bought from you
- **Frequency** - how frequently they buy from you
- **Value (£)** - at each point and overall

Successful companies tend to define a small number of segments from which they construct their CRM strategies.

Segments are increasingly dynamic as life events (described on previous page) take over from life stages as a means of profiling and predicting needs.

DIFFERING CRM THEMES & START POINTS

PREDICTIVE MODELLING

Putting customers into segments won't guarantee future behaviour. However, this can be anticipated with the aid of various predictive modelling techniques. Key drivers in predictive modelling include:

- Stated intention to repurchase (often derived from questionnaires) - eg: new car, to be purchased August 2001, budget £16,000
- Past purchase history
- Satisfaction with product/service
- Level of dissatisfaction/customer complaints

Predictive modelling is useful for making customer-related investment decisions. Fundamental to successful modelling is quality data.

DIFFERING CRM THEMES & START POINTS

VALUE SEGMENTATION

Putting customers into segments and predicting future value should drive CRM strategies.
Below is an illustrative example of six customer segments and the corresponding strategies.

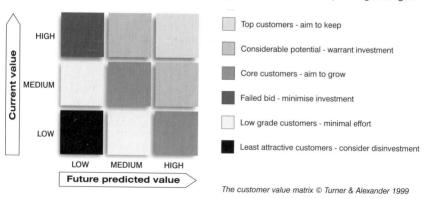

Top customers - aim to keep

Considerable potential - warrant investment

Core customers - aim to grow

Failed bid - minimise investment

Low grade customers - minimal effort

Least attractive customers - consider disinvestment

The customer value matrix © Turner & Alexander 1999

44

THE DIFFERENT ROLES PLAYED IN A CRM PROGRAMME

THE DIFFERENT ROLES PLAYED IN A CRM PROGRAMME

CRM A BUSINESS RESPONSIBILITY

Without customers an organisation will not survive. Therefore, the strategy for developing your business and servicing the needs of your valuable customers should be the catalyst for a CRM programme across your organisation.

A properly planned CRM programme demands the creation of a cross-functional team with CEO and wider executive-level sponsorship. This will ensure that the organisation focuses on how people, systems and processes need to be integrated in order to deliver the customer promise and the business result.

This section covers the roles different elements of the organisation can play. Marketing and information technology services are described in detail since many failed CRM programmes start here. The cause of failure varies but a common theme is lack of understanding of the wider context of CRM.

Thumb nail sketches of the roles of human resources, finance and administration, sales, support, and research and development are provided.

MARKETING IN A CRM PROGRAMME

The role of marketing breaks down into three key areas:

- To be the customer advocate
- To be an effective communications vehicle that will bring each area of the business together and ensure everyone understands CRM
- To apply the right mix of marketing techniques that meets the business objectives

THE DIFFERENT ROLES PLAYED IN A CRM PROGRAMME

MARKETING

THE CUSTOMER ADVOCATE

Ideally placed to operate cross-functionally within the organisation, marketing pulls together details of the customer from within the organisation and directly from the customer through a wide range of feedback mechanisms.

Key questions that should be asked on behalf of the customer about an approach, service, product or output from the CRM programme are:

- Will the customer value it and, if so, how much?
- Will the customer find it easy/convenient to use?
- Will the customer differentiate positively between their experience with us/our competitors?
- Will the deliverables from the CRM programme meet our target customer expectations?
- Is the proposed time-scale in line with the customer expectations?

Failure to test the CRM programme with these types of questions could lead you to deliver something that customers don't want.

THE DIFFERENT ROLES PLAYED IN A CRM PROGRAMME

MARKETING

EFFECTIVE COMMUNICATIONS

CRM affects all areas of the business, the customers, suppliers and investors. It brings significant change for an organisation and people can easily become uncomfortable or feel left out of the process.

It is essential that marketing provides a conduit for communication across each group, using the following guiding principles:

- Communicate frequently in bite-size chunks
- Make the message relevant to each different audience
- Provide a mechanism for open feedback
- Say what you mean, mean what you say
- Be open and succinct
- Demonstrate benefits to each audience type throughout the programme - **don't leave the success story until the end: you will have lost them!**

THE DIFFERENT ROLES PLAYED IN A CRM PROGRAMME

MARKETING
EXPLAIN WHAT CRM IS

In any organisation terminology becomes confused. One of the most common confusions is between Direct Marketing and Customer Relationship Management.

Direct Marketing
- Marketing activity based on customer knowledge built from customer data
- Direct marketing campaigns to acquire, retain and grow customers, and to cross-sell to them
- Marketing channels to support: help lines; web

Customer Relationship Management
- Business-wide commitment not just marketing, **cross-functional**
- Business organised around customers **not products**
- Single view of customer across all touch points, **technology challenge**
- Multi-channel delivery of goods, information **process**
- Relevant dialogue across all touch points, **communication**

Use the definitions in this pocketbook to help build your communications plan.

THE DIFFERENT ROLES PLAYED IN A CRM PROGRAMME

MARKETING

SHIFT IN EMPHASIS NEEDED

CRM is driving the development of **marketing techniques** to meet
the needs of two-way dialogue with customers across many touch
points. Traditional techniques are still of value but must be
integrated into a planned mix. Key challenges are to:

- Understand the different types of touch points your
  customers use (the range has increased dramatically)
- Know how to apply direct marketing techniques across
  the different touch points and customer segments
- Create a truly consistent message and integrated
  campaign to ensure consistency of experience
- Achieve effective marketing in an operational CRM
  programme through the synthesis of established
  and new marketing techniques

(51)

MARKETING

THE CHALLENGE

The marketing challenge under CRM is to identify the optimum way of utilising the wide range of techniques and channels to develop profitable customer relationships across multiple touch points in line with business objectives.

The direct communication mix model © Turner & Alexander 1998

THE DIFFERENT ROLES PLAYED IN A CRM PROGRAMME

MARKETING

EIGHT AREAS OF RESPONSIBILITY

All CRM programmes should have a marketing contribution covering the following areas:

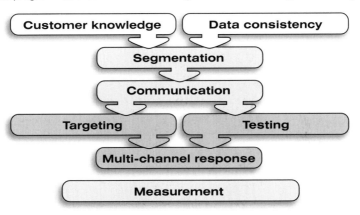

THE DIFFERENT ROLES PLAYED IN A CRM PROGRAMME

MARKETING

STRATEGY FOR BUILDING CUSTOMER KNOWLEDGE

All successful relationships require knowledge. Marketing within a CRM programme will build customer knowledge through:

- Questionnaires, online and offline
- Transactional data
- Reply forms and cards
- Capturing details of all customer interactions

Key questions for your marketing department to address are:

- What is our company's CRM knowledge strategy over multiple touch points?

- What knowledge will drive future company performance?

THE DIFFERENT ROLES PLAYED IN A CRM PROGRAMME

MARKETING

DATA CONSISTENCY & USE

One of the greatest challenges concerns data quality. Where data is collected at multiple touch points (web, direct mail, call centres, etc) there must be consistency. Key questions to address are:

- What is the overall strategy for collecting customer data?
- How can this knowledge be consistently collected?
- How will it be analysed to further understand customer needs and behaviour?
- Does the IT department understand how customer data is used in marketing and across the organisation?

THE DIFFERENT ROLES PLAYED IN A CRM PROGRAMME

MARKETING

CUSTOMER SEGMENTATIONS

Different customers have different values/worth to a company. Marketing's role is to take these segments and develop marketing programmes that generate loyalty and longer-term profitability.

For example, airlines run loyalty programmes in which the best customers get:

- Superior service (fast check-ins, last to board)
- Executive lounges
- Privileged partner offers
- Reward points
- Greater recognition
- Better support services (eg: call centres)

How will the marketing to customer segments be treated within your overall CRM strategy?

THE DIFFERENT ROLES PLAYED IN A CRM PROGRAMME

MARKETING
COMMUNICATION

Communication is one of the greatest challenges in a truly multi-channel CRM organisation. The range and breadth of communication possibilities have grown exponentially.

CRM communication can be real-time, anytime, multi-channel:

- Mobile, net, kiosk, call centre, e-mail, retail, etc

Marketing needs to consider:

- How brand values can be maintained across all channels
- Consistency of message

MARKETING

MEDIA SELECTION & TARGETING

One of marketing's key objectives is to target the right people, with the right message, at the right time. With the vast improvements in front office technology, which link and manage all touch points, the opportunity now exists to:

- Develop strategies to target and enhance relationships with customers across multiple channels

- Tailor the communication vehicle according to customer preferences (eg: one customer prefers to get their bank statement by e-mail, another by post)

- Create marketing campaigns based on a complete customer history

THE DIFFERENT ROLES PLAYED IN A CRM PROGRAMME

MARKETING

TESTING

Testing different alternatives is a classic marketing approach to determining the most effective ways of communicating with your customers.

Within your CRM programme, consider the opportunity to plan, test and improve across:

- Multi-channel communication links
- Multi-channel response mechanisms
- Different customer segments
- Different support services/support levels

MARKETING

MULTI-CHANNEL RESPONSE

CRM programmes, by their nature, encourage customers to talk back to you. This will involve marketing assessing and planning all response options. Customers' expectations are now much higher. For instance, in 1998 people would expect mail order deliveries to be made within 28 days. In 2001 their expectation is closer to three days. You need to consider all response options:

- Mail
- Phone
- Website
- E-mail
- Multiple channels
- Different options for different segments

THE DIFFERENT ROLES PLAYED IN A CRM PROGRAMME

MARKETING
MEASUREMENT

In order to assess the return on investment of marketing initiatives, marketing must develop customer profitability measures such as:

- Customer lifetime value modelling (What is a customer or customer segment worth to you during their lifetime with you?)

- Profitability measures by customer segment

- Customer satisfaction measures over multiple touch points

THE DIFFERENT ROLES PLAYED IN A CRM PROGRAMME

INFORMATION TECHNOLOGY SERVICES

Customer Relationship Management is not a technology programme. Many unsuccessful CRM programmes have failed to take account of this. Summarised below and on the following pages is a clear *terms of reference* for the information technology services function in your organisation.

Terms of reference
The role of an organisation's information technology services team (whether provided internally or by a service provider) must be focused on:

- Delivering the information services required to meet the business objectives within an agreed business plan and service level

- Delivering a consistent customer experience - at the right time, anywhere across the required touch points - by providing information services that are easy-to-use, customer-friendly and appropriate

- Being the organisation's advocate and protecting the business from vendor-driven technology initiatives that seek to make CRM a technology project only

THE DIFFERENT ROLES PLAYED IN A CRM PROGRAMME

INFORMATION TECHNOLOGY SERVICES

Terms of reference (cont'd)

- Providing effective innovation, advice, guidance and risk assessment on the possible approaches and implications of meeting business requirements in the areas of:
  - data collection, storage and retrieval
  - information services delivery to internal/external customers and users
  - integration of data, information services and software applications, to deliver a seamless view of and service to the customer
  - performance and capacity requirements of information services, to accommodate planned business activity and transaction volumes

- Ensuring the information services are designed, built and operated with the correct levels of resilience, scalability, serviceability, flexibility and availability

- Seeking out and recommending standards and open frameworks that protect the organisation from punitive technology lock-in that will inhibit business development in the future

THE DIFFERENT ROLES PLAYED IN A CRM PROGRAMME

INFORMATION TECHNOLOGY SERVICES

Terms of reference (cont'd)

- Acting as the guardians of the information assets of the organisation by maintaining detailed dictionaries of data available, business processes, software specifications, performance and utilisation information on transactions, data growth, processes and integration, and reliability

- Making sure that security policy/practice is in place and operating effectively to protect organisations and customer data in line with best practice and legislative obligations

HUMAN RESOURCES

CRM programmes inherently lead to a requirement for change management. Changes affect both people and processes. Having an effective HR support function as part of the programme enables the business strategy and subsequent CRM initiative to be translated into action in the following areas:

- Organising focus groups to secure employee feedback on proposed plans
- Assisting people to develop cross-functional teamworking skills
- Ensuring team profile is optimal for the programme requirements
- Ensuring ongoing development of job descriptions and competency frameworks that underpin the change programme
- Developing a training and development programme that brings people on
- Assisting in the realignment of people to support strategy and organise around the customer
- Recruiting people utilising new strategy and philosophy of the CRM programme

THE DIFFERENT ROLES PLAYED IN A CRM PROGRAMME

FINANCE & ADMINISTRATION

Finance & Administration, more than any other area, can **destroy** a CRM programme through a fundamental focus on short-term performance. A balance between medium- and long-term strategy and tactical short-term financial control is vital. Unfortunately, this is rarely achieved.

Securing involvement of Finance & Administration can reap significant rewards in the following areas:

- Development of the business plan as part of a cross-functional team
- Effective financial modelling of return on investment and tracking benefits realisation initiatives
- Accurate accounting for programme investment and expenditure, for understanding the programme scope and budget, and for assessment of the impact of change controls
- Driving process change with business processes to ensure customer focus and effectiveness

THE DIFFERENT ROLES PLAYED IN A CRM PROGRAMME

SALES

Sales people are the coalface of customer interactions. Probably more than any other group, sales can reap significant reward from a CRM programme:

- Reduced administration
- More time spent on selling and planning sales strategy
- Increased productivity and return on investment through effective collaboration

Regrettably, many CRM programmes are viewed negatively by sales. Why? Simply because they are not sold the benefits of the programme. Instead, they are told to invest significant time capturing the knowledge they hold in their heads or locally.

THE DIFFERENT ROLES PLAYED IN A CRM PROGRAMME

SALES

Sales' key role in a CRM programme is to:

- Secure, at every opportunity, intelligence about the customer and market, and ensure this information is fed into the CRM programme

- Ensure information gathered is analysed and acted on in an appropriate way, to secure increased business and customer satisfaction from the right customers and prospects

- Ensure that real-time feedback is gained from the coal-face regarding customer issues and requirements, to aid in the strategic planning of the business

Sales will behave according to the way they are remunerated and set goals. Successful CRM programmes take this into account and reward good behaviour.

THE DIFFERENT ROLES PLAYED IN A CRM PROGRAMME

SUPPORT

Customers see an organisation as one entity and expect to be treated as one customer. Unfortunately, with multiple channels many companies are failing to deliver a robust, consistent service. Support must:

- Provide consistent service levels across all customer touch points
- Take responsibility for customers at each of these points
- Implement and improve standards
- Ensure that the service is being delivered through constant testing such as mystery experience exercises. This is a marketing research programme that tests all typical customer experiences at all touch points on a regular basis.

THE DIFFERENT ROLES PLAYED IN A CRM PROGRAMME

RESEARCH & DEVELOPMENT

Classical research is often inaccurate as it asks **all** customers what they want rather than those customers who deliver the value to the business. Not surprisingly, the serial switcher always suggests better price, longer offer period or simply more for less.

A CRM programme genuinely enables R&D to:

- Secure real information about real customers and markets

- Drive product development from a customer-centric approach

- Orchestrate dynamic feedback between the customer and the whole organisation

- Develop better products and services that meet the needs of the customers the organisation is trying to attract, retain and develop

- Develop processes to ensure it constantly evaluates the information collected within a CRM programme, to learn what it needs to do and by when

- Proactively consider what information it needs and how it will be used

THE DIFFERENT ROLES PLAYED IN A CRM PROGRAMME

INVESTOR RELATIONS

That part of the organisation which manages investor relations needs to see CRM in the context of a communications challenge.

It is vital that you keep investors informed and supportive of a CRM initiative. If they do not understand CRM then they may well create pressure for ceasing investment in favour of short-term gains.

There are many types of investors. Let's look at the main ones as they all have different drivers. These are:

- Stock Exchange investors
- Private business investors
- Investors in not-for-profit organisations

THE DIFFERENT ROLES PLAYED IN A CRM PROGRAMME

INVESTOR RELATIONS

STOCK EXCHANGE INVESTORS

If you are listed on a stock exchange you will have a mixture of institutional investors and private investors. They have very different agendas.

Institutional investors are probably the holders of the majority of stock. They must be on side. Managing the message to their analysts is vital. They are generally cynical of strategic investment or the promise of jam tomorrow unless announcing it will improve the share price or earnings.

Private investors fall into two groups:

- Large private investors: can create mayhem for a business if they are not bought in; rarely are they there for the long-term

- Small investors: invariably speculate on share price growth

Lifestyle investors invest because they believe in your business and want to be part of its success over a long period. They can be large or small shareholders. Either way they are advocates and can be great advocates of CRM investments.

THE DIFFERENT ROLES PLAYED IN A CRM PROGRAMME

INVESTOR RELATIONS
STOCK EXCHANGE INVESTORS

As stated, Stock Exchange investors have different agendas. It is important to understand this when communicating strategy and investment decisions as you may be required to set it in a different context.

Investors seeking capital growth only care about an increase in share price which favours the short-term approach. Invariably, any investment that may delay this is seen negatively.

- Focus on competitive advantage, increased sales, customer retention/growth, and improved bottom line performance

Investors seeking income annually are investing their capital in a business because it promises to pay dividends on an annual basis. This dividend is used as income. Typically pension funds and investment funds aimed at delivering income represent the majority of investors along with small investors. Any investment that reduces the income will be viewed negatively.

- Focus on improved earnings per share, life-time value of customers, improved operational effectiveness and bottom line performance, and strengthened balance sheet

THE DIFFERENT ROLES PLAYED IN A CRM PROGRAMME

INVESTOR RELATIONS

PRIVATE BUSINESS INVESTORS

Private businesses are usually owned by a small group of people who are either directly linked to the business operationally, private investors with real interest or they or their family were at some time in the past involved in the business.

- CRM can be more readily understood in this environment as the long-term health of the business is seen as important as well as day-to-day hygiene issues

- Most businesses of this nature understand the value of individual customers and invariably show a better understanding of what makes the business profitable

- Securing their support is as vital as securing boardroom approval since dissatisfaction can lead rapidly to demands for change

THE DIFFERENT ROLES PLAYED IN A CRM PROGRAMME

INVESTOR RELATIONS

INVESTORS IN NOT-FOR-PROFIT ORGANISATIONS

These organisations, whether charity, trust or public sector, are faced with the dual challenge of raising money for worthy causes while at the same time appearing frugal in how they run the operation.

- Many of their stakeholders and regular contributors do not understand strategic investments in the operational aspect of the business unless they are related directly to the cause the organisation has been set up to support

- CRM in this arena is multi-faceted as the organisation needs to manage relationships with the principal donators of resources, the people who volunteer to raise the money or deliver the good works, and the people who sponsor their activities or receive the benefits

NOTES

PLANNING A CRM
<u>PROGRAMME</u>

NOW START PLANNING

The previous sections have provided answers to questions such as:

- What is customer relationship management?
- Why is it important in today's environment?
- What different models and themes are there?
- What are the different roles played within an organisation?

With this knowledge you are now in a position to develop
a CRM programme plan and business case.

CRM PLANNING PROCESS

There are five key stages to the CRM planning process:

1. **Undertake a CRM audit** - Identify how feasible it is to undertake CRM within your organisation and compare your position within your own market.

2. **Identify customer financial value** - How valuable are different groups of customers? What money should you invest? What return will you get?

3. **Establish the CRM vision** - Visualise the long-term picture of the future, what you want your relationship to be with your customers in the years ahead.

4. **Define the scope of CRM** - Determine how broadly you can employ CRM within your organisation. What are the individual projects that contribute to the CRM programme, that deliver the vision?

5. **Develop the business case** - Gain sign off from your board.

PLANNING A CRM PROGRAMME

AUDIT - THE RATIONALE

How can you know where you are going if you don't know where you are or came from?

An audit will help you understand the status quo and answer key questions:

- What is the current understanding of CRM?
- What is the current level of customer focus across the organisation?
- How important is it?
- What are the barriers to CRM being implemented?
- How will you get buy in and support?
- How can you drive CRM forward?

INTERNAL AUDIT - APPROACH

- Provide a clear definition and rationale for CRM
- Identify highly experienced representatives from Sales, Marketing, Service, Finance & Administration, Information Technology Services, Human Resources and Research & Development
- Conduct a series of one to one interviews using questionnaires and topic guides
- Gain insights from key people in the organisation, taking your total market into account (eg: UK, Europe, World)

INTERNAL AUDIT - OUTPUTS

Gain an understanding in each area:

- The processes around the customers
- The way of working
- The culture, mindset and attitude
- The systems
- The pain and stress points
- The parts of the process that are bureaucratic rather than customer focused

PLANNING A CRM PROGRAMME

EXTERNAL AUDIT - IDENTIFY CUSTOMER TOUCH POINTS

How many different ways can a customer touch your organisation? There are:

- Buying touch points
- Communication touch points
- Customer service touch points
- Customer generated touch points - informal routes into an organisation (eg: complaints)

Consider duplication and distribution of touch points (eg: four call centres, two internet sites). Assess usage and importance of each.

EXTERNAL AUDIT - OUTPUTS

- Identify the customer experience at each touch point (Mystery experience exercise by touch point).

- Grade by:
  - ability to handle query
  - level of customer sensitivity
  - how customers are moved to another part of the organisation.

- Assess what improvements can be made short-term and longer-term. What impact will this have on other departments?

PLANNING A CRM PROGRAMME

CRM MANAGEMENT QUESTIONS

- What are the true business benefits of CRM?
- How does CRM drive a company's financial performance?
- Which CRM capabilities have the most financial impact and warrant investment?

To answer these questions you NEED to apply customer lifetime value modelling.

RATIONALE FOR CUSTOMER LIFETIME VALUE

All customers are not equal in their future value to your business - some may even lose money. Thus, you need to calculate customer lifetime value.

CRM strategies aim to increase profitability through improved customer management.

Customer lifetime value is, therefore, the backbone of any CRM strategy:

- Who should you serve?
- How should you serve them?
- What will be their return on investment?

Applicable for both consumer and business markets.

CALCULATING LIFETIME VALUE

Prospects and customers participate in a multitude of 'events' throughout their lifetime with an organisation:

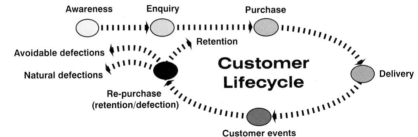

You must identify every event
during a customer's lifecycle. Allocate revenues
and costs against each event. Calculate the propensity
for each event to occur at future time periods. Create a profit & loss forecast.

DEVELOPING A VISION

With a clear understanding of the organisation and its customers (how they currently interact with you and their value) you are now in a position to create a vision. A CRM vision is a clear picture of how a company will be organised to serve its customers in the future. Key questions to consider in developing a vision are:

- What will our future customers want in five years' time? How do they want to deal with us in the future? What is their value/potential?
- How will they be using the new tools of society to manage their relationship?
- What will their expectations be of our company?
- What is the gap between our current offering and future expectations?

The vision must be supported with an outline of how your company should be structured in order to meet the needs of the future customer.

MAKING THE VISION A REALITY

The vision is the picture of the future. This may be five or ten years away. Its purpose is to provide a focus.

There are many CRM steps/projects on the road to meeting the vision.

Your challenge is to identify incremental steps.

How can we break the vision down into deliverables/projects? We do this by defining the scope of CRM.

DEFINING THE SCOPE OF CRM

The scope of CRM is huge. Attempting to do too much can result in doing nothing.

Identify the 'quick wins', those areas that are:

- Cost-efficient
- Easy to gain buy in
- Easy to implement
- Easy to measure

Use success to build success.

DEFINING THE SCOPE OF CRM

SET PRIORITIES

Short-term - quick wins
Example: 'call me' button on a website that links the site to a customer service centre.

Medium-term - pilot/annual projects
Example: audit and integration of all marketing databases.

Long-term
Example: company-wide re-organisation that dispenses with product departments in preference to customer segment departments.

Your challenge is to identify the benefits and expertise needed by project areas.

CREATING THE BUSINESS PLAN

Remember, CRM is a business initiative not just marketing.

Start with your company business objectives:

- What are the stated objectives?
- What is the strategy outlined in the annual report?

How will your CRM plan support the business objectives?

PLANNING A CRM PROGRAMME

CREATING THE BUSINESS PLAN

The following structure provides a practical format for delivering a board level CRM plan.

1. **Background to the future (CRM)**
   Portrait of your future customers:
   - What will their needs be?
   - How will they want to deal with you/your competition?
   - What are the risks of doing nothing?

2. **CRM vision**
   The long-term vision of the future that encapsulates how you will meet
   future customer needs.

3. **CRM objectives**
   These need to be quantifiable. What specific objectives are you trying to achieve?
   - Increase in customer retention? Increase in customer value?
   - What impact should this deliver on the bottom line?

CREATING THE BUSINESS PLAN

4. **Situation analysis**
   - Your company. This provides a snapshot of what you found from the internal audit.
   - Customer experience. This provides a snapshot of what you found from the external audit.
   - Competitor analysis. How does your customer management compare with that of your competitors?

5. **Practical CRM initiatives**
   - Short-term (in outline). Provide the quick wins. These are lower cost initiatives that improve the customer experience and can be easily justified.
   - Medium-term (broad brush). These projects will require significantly more input from other areas of the business and should only be presented in outline.

PLANNING A CRM PROGRAMME

CREATING THE BUSINESS PLAN

6. **Resource areas**
   Which departments need to deliver what?

7. **Initial budget**
   Anticipated costs that will be incurred for the first projects.

8. **Time lines**
   When you will achieve the earlier projects.

9. **Financial model/CLTV**
   Demonstration of return on investment from initiatives using business models.

10. **Critical success factors**
    What are the key things that measure the overall success of this project?

Executive Summary is a key deliverable.

EXECUTIVE SUMMARY IS KEY

Every business plan must have an executive summary.
In one page the CRM executive summary
should cover:

- The key reasons behind CRM
- The vision and key business objectives
- What you are intending to do
- Costs and return on investment

GAINING BUY IN FROM THE BOARD

- Pre-sell to line director/co-ownership with line director
  - gain approval for initial audits
  - get communication at board level: reasons/benefits to organisation

- Set expectations for board
  - understand the business benefits of pursuing CRM

- Board presentation = Executive Summary with pictures
  - less is more

- Aim to get senior management buy in to vision
  - agree CRM is right for organisation
  - agree initial programme, projects and budgets, and timetable

SPONSORSHIP IS CRITICAL

- CEO sponsorship
  - This is a must. It is a business issue responsibility that transcends divisions, departments and demarcation lines of all types

- Board representation responsibility
  - Facilitates cross-department working
  - Gains/protects budget/resource

- CRM has to be higher than inter-company politics

- CRM cannot be switched on and off

IMPLEMENTING A CRM PROGRAMME

IMPLEMENTING A CRM PROGRAMME

CRM IS A JOURNEY & WAY OF LIFE

As stressed throughout this book, CRM is an ongoing programme supported by a number of projects. The diagram below will help you visualise the overall programme. An explanation of each element is given on the following pages.

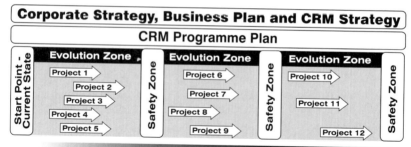

CRM PROGRAMME PLAN EXPLAINED

Corporate Strategy, Business Plan and CRM Strategy
The CRM strategy flows from the corporate strategy and business plan which lie at the heart of a business.

CRM Programme Plan
This is directly linked, via CRM strategy, to the corporate strategy and business plan. The CRM programme plan is built off the CRM strategy. It is best to think of the CRM programme plan in terms of a tour or journey with specific stages or adventures along the way. Summarised next are the key elements:
- Start point
- Evolution zones
- Safety zones
- Projects
- Time and funding

IMPLEMENTING A CRM PROGRAMME

CRM PROGRAMME PLAN EXPLAINED

Start point

All journeys start somewhere; yours starts with audit and planning work discussed in 'Planning a CRM Programme'.

Safety zones

Critically, there are points in time where you can clearly state what the organisation will look like after a series of projects have been implemented or steps taken. Safety zones allow you to review progress, tune the overall programme plan if circumstances have changed and demonstrate business results. They are an end state in their own right and can be described in business terms such as:

- 'We know who our customers are and how much they are worth to us in the future'
- 'We have identified all customer-centric processes and mapped them across the business'
- 'We have increased retention of valuable customers by XX%'

IMPLEMENTING A CRM PROGRAMME

CRM PROGRAMME PLAN EXPLAINED

Evolution zone
This is a period of time between the start point/safety zone and the subsequent safety zone. During the period (usually no more than six months) several projects, which may be interconnected, can be in operation.

Projects
These are time limited. In short, they start and finish and have specific measurable, attainable, relevant and trackable outputs. A team is put together for the specific duration and released at the end. Projects cannot be interconnected across evolution zones.

Time and Funding
A programme runs over years. This means that budgets and planning across the organisation need to make provision for this, year on year. It is simply the cost of doing business.

IMPLEMENTING A CRM PROGRAMME

WHERE STRATEGY TRANSLATES INTO ACTION

Your planning is vital but eventually the time comes when your programme needs to be implemented. People are the key to success: this, after all, is as much about change management as anything. So, let's summarise what you need before you start:

- **CEO sponsorship** - The CEO must understand it, be able to clearly state what the vision and requirement are, and be prepared to take executive action.

- **Programme Director Champion** - Someone with clout (eg: respected operational board director) who is prepared to take responsibility for delivering against business objectives. The individual will be accountable to the board and no one else.

THE PROGRAMME MANAGER

The Programme Manager - who is accountable only to the project champion, and who has a broad knowledge of the organisation - is responsible for the day-to-day management of the project team, for progress chasing and for assessing risk. Can call on the CEO when needed.

Attributes of a Programme Manager:
- Solid project management skills
- Able to focus on deliverables and keep on plan
- Fearless - not afraid to say how it is and to escalate issues when required
- Good communicator
- Ruthless attention to detail
- A completer/finisher, monitor/evaluator

(105)

IMPLEMENTING A CRM PROGRAMME

CRM PROGRAMME TEAM

Your CRM programme team must comprise the best people in your organisation.
This poses challenges to your management team, to release people to work on the
CRM programme. Do not let it become a dumping ground for poor performers.
The programme team needs to be:

- A small group of individuals released from their day jobs
- Drawn from each area of the business - Marketing, IT, Sales, Support, R&D, Legal,
  Finance & Administration
- Made up of people who bring real knowledge/expertise of their area

Each of the members needs management support and special training to enable them to
work in a small team and drive change. They require:

- Help to form a team and training in cross-functional teamworking, change
  management and programme/project management
- Empowerment to make change happen

CRM PROGRAMME PLAN

CRITICAL SUCCESS FACTORS

- **Focus on outputs** - Don't focus on the process. Process is a tool to deliver the result, not an end in itself.

- **Execute an ongoing communication plan** - This should be aimed at all stakeholders, be they customers, investors, employees or suppliers. It should focus on benefits expected, route to achieving them and the role people can play in making the CRM programme happen. Different emphasis and depth for each audience are required.

- **Fail to prepare, prepare to fail!** - You would not start building a house or set out on a flight if you had no blueprint or flight plan. Plans are living things, they need constant updating and monitoring. They should be the key tool for determining the status of the programme or projects. **Plan your work and work your plan!**

CRM PROGRAMME PLAN

CRITICAL SUCCESS FACTORS

- **Select the right tools for the job** - And make sure they are used:
  - adopt a programme management method appropriate to your business
  - adopt a project management method appropriate to your business

- **Develop the programme and project teams** - Profile your team for strengths and areas for development. Then train them in:
  - listening skills
  - negotiating skills
  - presentation and communication skills
  - planning skills

- **Remember the sequence** - Design, plan, build, implement and then operate. This simple reminder will provide a sanity check at any stage of a project or the overall programme. Too many projects have ended up on the rocks because people tried to bypass these basic steps.

CRM PROGRAMME PLAN

CRITICAL SUCCESS FACTORS

- **Control plan changes** - Establish formal change control and approval processes across the programme and projects. Failure to do this will sink your programme and people will never understand the consequences of requests for changes.
  - beware the minor change requests by senior management; they are time bombs
  - there are three dimensions which are linked in a project …
    time - available to deliver work
    resources - available to do work
    specification - amount of work to do
    … they must all be in balance

- **Have contingency plans and quality standards** - Focus on doing it right first time. But, as we all know, things rarely go exactly to plan, so ensure you have flexibility and contingency built in. This means exploring proactively what the problems could be and how you would respond to them.

CRM PROGRAMME

CHECKLIST

- **Focus on customers** - Remember, this is about customers so focus on what they want and ensure someone is acting as the customer advocate at all times. Prioritise by customer need and return on investment.

- **Walk the talk** - Ensure fulfilment and delivery keep up with aspiration and expectation set within the organisation and among customers. Delight, out-perform, never fail to meet expectations.

- **Make sure it scales, is reliable, flexible and easy to support** - No matter whether it is IT, call centre, delivery or support it must be able to evolve to meet your business plans. Too often organisations cut corners and make short-term decisions that ultimately undermine the CRM programme.

- **Plan for success** - Don't let your organisation pay lip service to CRM. It is better not to start at all. If you cannot get the right team or the right budget then recommend that your organisation does not even start.

AN EXAMPLE
PROJECT METHOD

AN EXAMPLE PROJECT METHOD

BALANCED APPROACH

There are many ways of undertaking a project. The six-stage approach described on the following pages can be used as a generic template. It balances the range of issues involved in developing solutions for the effective delivery of a CRM programme. It ensures you can:

- De-risk your projects
- Link projects back to the CRM programme clearly
- Implement on an incremental basis
- Retain the overall vision for CRM within your organisation
- Apply early experiences to subsequent stages and projects
- Make effective use of your resources
- Operate a cross-company implementation with clear lines of responsibility

AN EXAMPLE PROJECT METHOD

GENERIC SUCCESS-FOCUSED PROJECT METHOD

Stage 1 - Resource Mobilisation
- Initiate project
- Initiate planning
- Set up infrastructure

Stage 2 - Project Kick-off
- Undertake detailed project planning - what/when/how task allocated
- Produce/approve project initiation document which outlines plans, milestones and deliverables
- Begin scoping exercises for project stages

AN EXAMPLE PROJECT METHOD

GENERIC SUCCESS-FOCUSED PROJECT METHOD

Stage 3 - Design
- Detail how business will be changed
    - define processes, inputs and outputs required
    - identify disconnects, interdependencies
- Prepare for interface development between systems and processes, including data conversion and data take on
- Deliver approved design documents for processes and systems

Stage 4 - Development, integration and initial testing
- Develop new services and processes, test against design documents
- Test each major component of the project
- Develop test plans and scripts to drive integrated testing of customer-centric processes

AN EXAMPLE PROJECT METHOD

GENERIC SUCCESS-FOCUSED PROJECT METHOD

Stage 5 - Implementation and full testing
- Involve all project team members
- Gain documented acceptance of test plans and scripts
- Obtain senior management approval of criteria for success
- Integrate systems, processes, third party interfaces with simulation of live environment

Stage 6 - User and customer training followed by go live and review
- Implement training courses on philosophy, processes, systems and individual role within delivering effective CRM (builds on communication programme)
- Provide ongoing help desk and support to customers and users during training and after new process or system goes live
- Following implementation, review, learn lessons, fine-tune future plans, make formal changes

About the Authors

David Alexander
David is a senior business professional and strategy consultant
who has operated in a board capacity in a number of roles.
His expertise across business functions, balanced with
meeting the City, shareholder and customer needs, has led
to thought leadership, clear vision and strategy development.

David currently mentors board directors, lectures and authors
books on key business issues. He is passionate about
putting customers at the centre of business strategy and
delivering value to the business.

Contact
David can be contacted at:
E-mail: david.alexander@cwcom.net

Charles Turner
Charles is a management consultant and leading authority
in customer relationship management. He writes many articles
and lectures on the subject across Europe.

His approach enables him to help organisations create a
CRM vision and translate this into a clear programme
for delivery.

In conjunction with David Alexander, he developed and
delivers the highly successful 'CRM for Marketers' course
at the Institute of Direct Marketing - a world renowned body.

Contact
Charles can be contacted at:
E-mail: charlesandrewturner@hotmail.com

POCKETBOOKS FOR THE MANAGER

- Instant reference or checklist for experienced managers

- No-nonsense, practical help for new managers

- Practical, easy-to-use aid for self-development

- Avoid time-consuming reading; get straight to the facts

- A series of Pocketbooks for the price of a textbook

POCKETBOOKS
FOR THE TRAINER

- Reinforce learning messages

- Back-up material for training workshops

- Help 'sell' training and hold interest in training 'queue'

- Professional, inexpensive alternative to in-house prepared course notes

- Written by leading training professionals

- Invaluable library material

THE MANAGEMENT POCKETBOOK SERIES

Pocketbooks

Appraisals
Assertiveness
Balance Sheet
Business Planning
Business Presenter's
Business Writing
Challengers
Coaching
Communicator's
Controlling Absenteeism
Creative Manager's
C.R.M.
Cross-cultural Business
Cultural Gaffes
Customer Service
Decision-making
Developing People
Discipline
E-commerce
E-customer Care

Empowerment
Facilitator's
Handling Complaints
Improving Efficiency
Improving Profitability
Induction
Influencing
Interviewer's
Key Account Manager's
Learner's
Managing Budgets
Managing Cashflow
Managing Change
Managing Your Appraisal
Manager's
Marketing
Meetings
Mentoring
Motivation
Negotiator's

Networking
People Manager's
Performance Management
Personal Success
Project Management
Problem Behaviour
Quality
Sales Excellence
Salesperson's
Self-managed Development
Starting In Management
Stress
Teamworking
Telephone Skills
Telesales
Thinker's
Time Management
Trainer Standards
Trainer's

Pocketsquares

Great Presentation Scandal
Great Training Robbery
Hook Your Audience
Leadership: Sharing The Passion

Pocketfiles

Trainer's Blue Pocketfile of
Ready-to-use Exercises
Trainer's Green Pocketfile of
Ready-to-use Exercises
Trainer's Red Pocketfile of
Ready-to-use Exercises

Audio Cassettes

Tips for Presenters
Tips for Trainers

ORDER FORM

Your details

Name _____

Position _____

Company _____

Address _____

_____

_____

Telephone _____

Facsimile _____

E-mail _____

VAT No. (EC companies) _____

Your Order Ref _____

Please send me:

		No. copies
The C.R.M.	Pocketbook	☐
The _____	Pocketbook	☐
The _____	Pocketbook	☐
The _____	Pocketbook	☐
The _____	Pocketbook	☐

Order by Post

MANAGEMENT POCKETBOOKS LTD
14 EAST STREET ALRESFORD HAMPSHIRE SO24 9EE UK

Order by Phone, Fax or Internet
Telephone: +44 (0)1962 735573
Facsimile: +44 (0)1962 733637
E-mail: sales@pocketbook.co.uk
Web: www.pocketbook.co.uk

Customers in USA should contact:
Stylus Publishing, LLC, 22883 Quicksilver Drive,
Sterling, VA 20166-2012
Telephone: 703 661 1581 or 800 232 0223
Facsimile: 703 661 1501 E-mail: styluspub@aol.com

Published by:
Management Pocketbooks Ltd
14 East Street, Alresford, Hants SO24 9EE, U.K.
Tel: +44 (0)1962 735573   Fax: +44 (0)1962 733637
E-mail: sales@pocketbook.co.uk
Website: www.pocketbook.co.uk

This edition published 2001

ISBN 1 870471 97 0

Design, typesetting and graphics by artsFX Ltd. Printed in U.K.

British Library Cataloguing-in-Publication Data – A catalogue record for this book is available from the British Library.